British Royal Commemoratives

THE FIRST-TIME COLLECTOR'S GUIDE TO

BRITISH ROYAL COMMEMORATIVES

GEOFFREY WARREN

THE
APPLE
PRESS

A QUINTET BOOK

Published by The Apple Press
6 Blundell Street.
London N7 9BH

ISBN 1–85076–504–9

This book was designed and produced by
Quintet Publishing Limited
6 Blundell Street
London N7 9BH

Creative Director: Richard Dewing
Designer: Pete Laws
Project Editor: Stefanie Foster
Photographer: Martin Norris

DEDICATION
For Peter

Typeset in Great Britain by
Central Southern Typesetters, Eastbourne
Manufactured in Singapore by
Eray Scan Pte. Ltd
Printed in Singapore by
Star Standard Industries Ptd. Ltd

ACKNOWLEDGEMENTS

The author and Quintet Publishing thank the following dealers and
private collectors for lending items:
BRITISH COLLECTABLES (Mr D. Colton), 9 Georgian Village,
Camden Passage, London, N1 8XE. Tel: 071 359 4560; Mr Robert
Borzello; Mr Robert Field; HOPE AND GLORY (Mr E. Titmuss),
131a Kensington Church Street, London, W8 7LP. Tel: 071 727 8424;
Mr Steven Jackson; Mr Raymond Lavender; MS ANTIQUES
(Mrs Swycher and Mr F. Swycher), 40 Gordon Place, Holland Street,
London, W8 4JF. Tel: 071 937 0793 (Staffordshire figures only);
RONALD A. SMITH, 7 Pierrepoint Row, Camden Passage, London,
N1 8XE. Tel: 071 226 8211; ROYAL DOULTON (Miss Valeris Baynton,
Museum and Tours Manager). A number of items are from the
author's own collection.
The author also thanks the following for their advice:
Mr David Drummond, Mr Robin Hunt, Mr Steven Jackson and
Mr Ernest Titmuss.

CONTENTS

INTRODUCTION

The British monarchy is not only one of the oldest in the world but one which has inspired more commemoratives than any other – offering a wide, rich and fascinating range of objects for the first-time collector.

Royal commemoratives were, and still are, bought by mainly everyday people to express loyalty and patriotism, through an interest in the Royal Family or to form a collection for its own sake. Such commemoratives give a unique glimpse and an insight into British history and heritage. Attractive and sometimes curious, they also reflect changes in taste, design and decoration over the years.

EARLY DAYS

Edgar, the first King of England, was crowned in 937 but the earliest known royal commemorative is a gold medal struck for the coronation of Edward VI in 1547.

Royal commemoratives were few and far between until the early 19th century though. However this did not necessarily indicate a lack of loyalty to the crown. Commemoratives had to be hand-made and decorated, and were therefore scarce; distribution methods were limited; there were difficulties in disseminating news – such as a coronation – and the population was in general poor and had no money to spare for "trifles".

THE FIRST ROYAL MUG

After Edward's reign there are no known Tudor commemoratives apart from another gold medal

struck to celebrate the defeat of the Spanish Armada in 1558 bearing a portrait of Elizabeth I, and a 1600 English delftware dish carrying a verse in praise of her. A medal was issued for the coronation of James I in 1603; this custom continues for coronations and other royal events up to the present day. Medals and engravings of monarchs were the only commemoratives available until Charles II came to the throne in 1660, when the first royal mug appeared, together with the first piece of glass and the first of a series of English and Dutch delftware ceramics. Intended for fairly sophisticated and wealthy people, the latter continued to be made; they bore rather crude portraits of the rest of the Stuart monarchs and the first three Georges.

COMMERCIALISM GETS UNDER WAY

In about 1759 George II made commemorative history by being the first monarch to have his portrait printed on a commercially available mug. George III's coronation in 1760 inspired a number of ceramic pieces, as did other events in his reign. Unpopular George IV staged the most lavish coronation of all, which prompted ceramic and other commemoratives; it was the first one at which free dinners were held and free gifts were given. By contrast, William IV's coronation in 1831 was a meagre affair but the public liked him and were happy to buy quite a number of prints, ceramics, the first commercially made royal busts and the first royal jigsaw puzzle.

Practically all the ceramic (and other) commemoratives therefore carry the "wrong" date, making the few with the "right" date rare and valuable. All the famous potteries continued to contribute and, to entice wealthy patriots or collectors, they introduced costly limited editions, a practice that continues today. Only a small number of ceramics was made to mourn Edward's death in 1910.

SUPERB LOVING CUPS

Among the many ceramics made for George V's coronation in 1911 is the first of Royal Doulton's elaborately moulded stoneware two-handled loving cups. For this event, the firm made a three-handled version, known as a tyg. Similar two-handled versions were issued for successive coronations, for George V's Silver Jubilee in 1935, and for Elizabeth II's Silver Jubilee in 1977. George V's Jubilee otherwise saw only some not very distinguished pieces. Only a few – though fine – ceramics record his death in 1936.

THE YEAR OF THE THREE KINGS, 1936

The coronation of the immensely popular Edward VIII, which was scheduled for 12 May 1936, inspired a great number of (mostly) attractive ceramics, some in the then-current Art Deco style. But as soon as he

abdicated on 11 December 1936, his brother, the Duke of York, automatically became George VI, an event which later occasioned a tyg, carrying portraits of the three monarchs (see page 14). The switch caused dismay in the royal commemorative industry. Some factories smashed their Edward VIII ware, some pieces never left the factory and Minton *gave* their items to their employees. Even so, contrary to popular myth, there are still many of the "proposed" coronation ceramics around which are no more expensive than those made for any other royal event.

Since George VI's coronation was to be held on 12 May 1937, manufacturers had to begin afresh in a great hurry, but succeeded in producing many fine ceramics in record time. Throughout his reign, ceramics were made to mark tours and visits (some cancelled due to the King's ill health), but none was made to register his death in 1952.

A PLETHORA OF EVENTS

Elizabeth's coronation in 1953 produced a welter of ceramics: some grand, some garish, others displaying the rather feeble "good taste" typical of the 1951 Festival of Britain. Among the most stylish of ceramics made for this coronation are Minton's large, orb-shaped powder bowls in white, turquoise and red, decorated with gold.

Although more royal events than ever have been marked by ceramic commemoratives since about 1978, they have been issued in smaller numbers than they used to be. Therefore some are not easy to find but all the more worth looking for.

Victoria

Queen Victoria's Golden Jubilee, 1887. On this mug the mob-capped Queen is set in a wreath of emblematic roses of England, thistles of Scotland and shamrocks of Ireland. By Tuscan Bone China. £120 ($180)

Queen Victoria's Golden Jubilee, 1887. The Prince of Wales – later Edward VII – paid for 45,000 of these sepia-printed pottery beakers, over 30,000 of which were distributed to schoolchildren gathered in Hyde Park in June for a fête which was attended by the Queen. By Doulton Burslem. £110 ($165)

Queen Victoria's Golden Jubilee, 1887. A rather crude sepia drawing of a regally dressed Queen decorates the front of this pottery mug. One side carries an appropriate inscription: the other relates that William Challinor opened the Leek Jubilee Festival in Staffordshire, held in the Pickwood Recreation Ground, where he gave a tea and this mug to 5,000 "scholars", meaning schoolchildren. Unmarked. £120 ($180)

Queen Victoria's Golden Jubilee, 1887. A pottery mug on which the Queen, bejewelled and wearing a coronet and a veil, is seen in a splendidly ornate setting. Unmarked. £75 ($110–115)

Queen Victoria's Diamond Jubilee, 1897. A beautifully moulded stoneware beaker displaying portraits of the young and old Queen; the design and colour are characteristic of the many ceramics made for this (and the 1887) Jubilee by Doulton, Lambeth. £150 ($225)

The death of Queen Victoria, 1901. A suitably black transfer of the Queen wearing her famous miniature crown, set in a wreath of English roses. An inscription on the reverse, in a similar wreath reads: "IN MEMORY of our Beloved Queen WHO DIED Jan. 22nd." Unmarked. £175 ($260–265)

EDWARD VII

The Coronation of Edward VII, 1902. A frequently used elaborate transfer showing both the King and Queen Alexandra is applied to this ripple-rimmed pottery mug. Continental. £48 ($70–75)

The Coronation of Edward VII, 1902. A splendidly regal Edward adorns this popular pottery mug. Weakened by his recent operation, the 59-year-old King wore the smaller version Imperial State Crown made for Queen Victoria, instead of the traditional, heavier, St. Edward's crown. Continental. £65 ($95–100)

GEORGE V

The Coronation of George V, 1911. This richly decorated pottery mug is interesting because it portrays not only a Highland soldier and a sailor, but also a portrait of the 17-year-old Prince of Wales, later Edward VIII and then the Duke of Windsor. Unmarked. £46 ($65–70)

The Silver Jubilee of George V, 1935. This pottery mug carries a conventional transfer but has a very unusual handle bearing a gilded crown and orb. By James Kent. £45

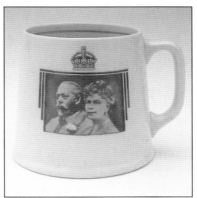

The Silver Jubilee of George V, 1935. Informal photographs of the King and Queen on a simple, uncomplicated pottery mug, in Art Deco style. A number of these inscribed mugs were given to patients in the Cheyne Hospital for Children in Chelsea, London. Royal Doulton. £42 ($60–65)

The death of George V, 1936. Often called "The Exemplar Loving Cup", this large china piece uses the same photograph of the King as on the previous mug, set in a mourning garland of leaves in low relief. The inscription on the reverse reads: "The Friend of his people. So long as the history of the British Empire is written, his reign will be recorded with gratitude. 1910–1936." By Royal Doulton. £160 ($240)

EDWARD VIII

The Coronation of George VI, 1937. An elegant pottery beaker showing the Royal Family set in a heart shape. By Wedgwood & Co Ltd. (Not to be confused with the better-known Wedgwood) £45 ($65–70)

The "Proposed" Coronation of Edward VIII, 1937. A beautiful example of Wedgwood's jasper ware, simple, elegant and finely modelled, one of the best ceramics made for this "non-event". £175 ($260–265)

The Year of the Three Kings, 1936. This large china tyg, or three-handled loving cup, carries portraits of George V who died on 20 January, Edward VIII who abdicated on 11 December and George VI who became King on the same day, a unique sequence of events in one year which makes this piece particularly interesting. Although made in 1937, it seems fitting to place it here, before the reign of George VI. By James Kent. £150

The Coronation of George VI, 1937. After the abdication of the unmarried Edward VIII, much was made of the fact that the country had a Royal Family; therefore, on this pottery mug the King is shown with Queen Elizabeth, Princess Elizabeth and Princess Margaret Rose in a photograph by Marcus Adams. By Royal Albert. £45 ($65–70)

The Coronation of George VI, 1937. This china mug was designed by Dame Laura Knight RA, an adaptation of the one she designed for Edward VIII's coronation. Famed for her paintings of circus life, she substituted a horse and an elephant for the Lion and the Unicorn on the Royal Arms. Note the lion's head on the handle. By Burleigh Ware. Deluxe edition with gilding, £175 ($260–265) "Ordinary" examples, £60 ($90)

The Coronation of George VI, 1937. A superb china loving cup with a stylish gold transfer on black, with gilded handles, rim and base. By Coalport. £95 ($140–145)

The State Tour of South Africa by George VI, Queen Elizabeth, Princess Elizabeth and Princess Margaret (Rose had been dropped by this time), 1947. The embossed portraits on this pottery mug are, by this date, in rather old-fashioned Art Deco style. It was on this tour that Princess Elizabeth celebrated her 21st birthday and made her famous speech in which she dedicated her life to the service of her country. By Vanguard. £45 ($65–70)

The Proposed Tour of Australia by George VI and Queen Elizabeth, 1949. A simple pottery mug with an appropriate koala on the handle. The tour was cancelled because of the King's ill health. By Bentleigh. £95 ($140–145)

The Coronation of Elizabeth II, 1953. The official pottery beaker, bearing a conventional transfer, which was given to schoolchildren by town councils and schools. Unmarked. £18 ($25–30)

The Coronation of Elizabeth II, 1953. When Wedgwood commissioned Professor Richard Guyatt to design this creamware pint-sized mug and others in similar style, they selected an artist of exceptional talent: the design is a lively, elegant and witty rendering of the Royal Arms, one of the most successful of all the ceramics made for this coronation. Since then, Professor Guyatt has designed similar, often more elaborately decorated, mugs for 14 other Royal occasions, all prized by collectors. £85 ($125–130)

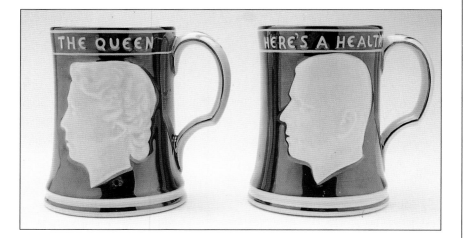

The Coronation of Elizabeth II, 1953. A pair of gold lustre tankards with white relief portraits. Around the rim of the Queen's a missive reads "THE QUEEN GOD BLESS HER"; around the Duke of Edinburgh "HERE'S A HEALTH TO THE DUKE" and on the reverse "WHOM GOD PRESERVE". By Ridgway. £50 ($75) the pair

The Coronation of Elizabeth II, 1953. This 26.7cm (10in)-high loving cup, made of saltglaze stoneware with carved, incised and modelled decoration, is one of the grandest made for this coronation. (Similar cups were made for George V's Silver Jubilee, the coronations of Edward VIII and George VI, and for Queen Elizabeth II's Silver Jubilee). The portrait, with a view of Windsor Castle in the background, is taken from a photograph by Dorothy Wilding, which was used for many commemoratives for this coronation. Since much was made of a "New Elizabethan Age", the reverse carries a portrait of Elizabeth I against a depiction of the Armada. By Royal Doulton. £300–400 ($450–600)
This may seem expensive for a first-time collector, but anyone who has this or one of the other cups has something really valuable!

The Coronation of Elizabeth II, 1953. A charming example of "art" pottery with slip decoration, made especially for "Trevor" whose name appears on the reverse. Unmarked. £12 ($15–20)

The Coronation of Elizabeth II, 1953. One of the prettiest of all china cups and saucers made for any royal event. (A similar design was made for Princess Margaret's wedding in 1960 – a much rarer, and much sought-after, piece). By Paragon. £28 ($40–45)

The Investiture of the Prince Wales, 1969. A smiling 21-year-old Prince is flanked by the Union Jack and the Welsh flag on this china mug with a gilt rim. By Coronet. £35 ($50–55)

The Silver Wedding of Queen Elizabeth II and the Duke of Edinburgh, 1972. A china mug with an elegant, simple design. By Crown Staffordshire, £34 ($50–55)

The Death of the Duke of Windsor, 1972. A china mug which carries a rather crude drawing of the Duke, with one of the Duchess on the reverse. On the side are printed the Duke's titles and an extract from the abdication speech from Shakespeare's *Richard II* which includes the line "With mine own hands I give away my crown." By Mercian. £185 ($275–280)

The Silver Wedding of Queen Elizabeth II and the Duke of Edinburgh, 1972. This china mug, with an appropriate silver rim, displays only the Royal Arms and an inscription in good calligraphy. By Wilson's of Paignton. £32 ($45–50)

The Wedding of Princess Anne and Captain Mark Phillips, 1973. This grand wedding held in Westminster Abbey was considered by the Queen to be a "private" and not a "state" affair. So by law no royal emblems were allowed on commemoratives, only portraits, as on this pottery mug, also cheerfully embellished with wedding bells. By Aynsley. £35 ($50–55)

The Wedding of Princess Anne and Captain Mark Phillips, 1972. A pottery mug strikingly decorated with a bold design of gold on black – even if the portraits are rather crudely drawn. By Portmeirion. £22 ($30–35)

The Silver Jubilee of Elizabeth II, 1977. A distinguished creamware pint-sized mug decorated with a photograph of the Queen by Lord Snowdon, who also designed the piece. The Queen wears George IV's 1821 State Diadem. As it is the crown she wears to and from the State Opening of Parliament and on all United Kingdom stamps and many coins, it is seen by more people than any other piece of royal jewellery. By Wedgwood. £20 ($30)

The Silver Jubilee of Elizabeth II, 1977. A pottery mug made for the popular market with a jolly, simple and bold design in patriotic red, white and blue. The reverse carries the first three lines of the National Anthem. By Adams. £6 ($9–10)

The Wedding of Prince Charles and Lady Diana Spencer, 1981. The half-smiling bride and groom appear on the front of this fine china mug. On the reverse the Prince's and Lady Diana's coats of arms are displayed. By Coalport. £38 ($55–60)

The Silver Jubilee of Elizabeth II, 1977. A pottery mug with one of the more popular, rather conventional, transfers showing the Queen and Prince Philip. Unmarked. £12 ($18–20)

The Wedding of Prince Charles and Lady Diana Spencer, 1981. An elegant china goblet, carrying relief portraits of the couple is, unusually, resting on a stand consisting of two beautifully sculpted bronze Welsh Dragons. Overall height 20.3cm (8in). By Albany Fine China. £120 ($180)

The 85th Birthday of Queen Elizabeth the Queen Mother, 1985. Commemoratives have been made to mark Her Majesty's birthdays since 1975, but this is one of the scarcest. A stylish china loving cup typical of Crown Derby's high standard of design and workmanship. £120 ($180)

The 40th Anniversary of Elizabeth II's accession to the throne, 1992. A broadly smiling Queen is surrounded by the national flowers of England, Scotland, Wales and Northern Ireland. Caverswall. £18 ($25–30)

The Wedding of Prince Charles and Lady Diana Spencer, 1981. The famous "ear" pottery mug; one of the first satirical royal ceramics. Since the Prince of Wales was Chairman of the Committee set up to vet the standard of commemoratives made for the wedding, members were fearful of his reaction, but he was delighted with it. The reverse carries the verse: "Whatever beverage brims this cup/Thank God for PRINCE CHARLES when you pick it up/ And as you quaff it, bless the same great Planner/Who gave him for bride the fair DIANA."
The design is based on a drawing by the late cartoonist "Marc", Mark Boxer. By Carlton. At the time it cost £1.50 ($2–2.50), now worth between £32 and £38 ($45 and $60)

The Birth of Prince William of Wales, 21 June 1982. A china mug with a pretty design incorporating photographs of the beaming Prince and Princess (their first child is second in line to the throne) and Victorian-style cupids. By Mayfair. £20 ($30)

The 40th Wedding Anniversary of Queen Elizabeth II and the Duke of Edinburgh, 1987. An informal photograph on a typical gilded and lion-decorated china beaker by Sutherland. £45 ($65–70)

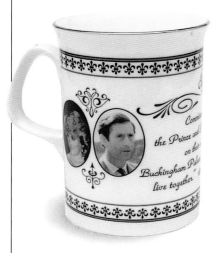

The Separation of the Prince and Princess of Wales, 18 December, 1992. A china mug to mark the separation of the couple. In the not-so-distant past such an event would not have occurred, let alone have been commemorated; it is a sign of the changing attitude towards the monarchy in some quarters. These black-and-white photographs are tinted pink as is the circular double portrait of the couple on the reverse. The front of the mug carries the inscription: "Commiserations to the Prince and Princess of Wales on their separation. Buckingham Palace – '. . . will no longer live together'" and the date. By Lady Grace China. £20 ($30)

The Divorce of Princess Anne and Captain Mark Phillips, 1992. A rather inappropriately smiling couple and separate photographs are on this china mug. The reverse displays a mock-up of the divorce document with Anne's signature. By Mayfair. £20 ($30)

Elizabeth II's *Annus Horribilis*, 1992. On 24 December, speaking at an official luncheon at the Guildhall in London to mark the 40th anniversary of her reign, the Queen admitted that it had been an *Annus Horribilis* or "horrible year" – and asked for public and media sympathy. On this china mug Her Majesty is surrounded by Christmas holly and ivy; the reverse carries a long, sympathetic verse. By J & S Chown. It retailed for £12.50 ($15–20), but by mid-1993 was worth £25 ($35–40)

The Great Fire at Windsor Castle, 20–21 November 1992. The blaze destroyed a large part of the building, including St George's Hall. This china mug also carries silhouettes of the Queen and the Duke of York (here named as HRH Prince Andrew) who helped to supervise the firemen. By Lady Grace China. £20 ($30)

This china mug is one of the souvenirs available to anyone who toured the State Apartments of Buckingham Palace when they were opened to the public for the first time on 7 August 1993. The 22-carat gold design is taken from a damask in the White Drawing Room which forms part of a suite of apartments designed by John Nash for George IV in the 1820s. By Royal Collections Enterprises Ltd. For sale at £10 ($15) but may well rise in value.

ℰDWARD VII

The Coronation of Edward VII, 1902. A modest pottery jug which shows Queen Alexandra wearing Queen Victoria's miniature crown; on the reverse is a drawing of Britannia. Unmarked. £45 ($65–70)

ℰLIZABETH II

The Coronation of Elizabeth II, 1953. A gloriously garish gold lustre jug with a gilded handle. By Sadler. £18 ($25–30)

The 40th Anniversary of Elizabeth II's Accession to the Throne, 1992. Toby jugs have been made since the 18th century and this modern pottery example, decorated with enamels, follows in this tradition. There is an element of, perhaps kindly, satire in the fact that the regally dressed Queen has a royal corgi sitting beside her. By Kevin Francis. £130 ($195). Figurative representations of the Queen have featured on other jugs. For her coronation in 1953, she is shown sitting on the Coronation Chair (by Burleigh Ware). To mark her Silver Jubilee in 1977, she is on horseback at the Trooping the Colour Ceremony (by Burgess and Leigh).

Another Toby jug, depicting the Princess of Wales wearing riding breeches, boots and coat sitting on a stone wall. By Kevin Francis. £115 ($170–175)

𝓔DWARD VIII

The "Proposed" Coronation of Edward VIII, 1937. A "Brown Betty" pottery teapot, gilded but with an "everyday" feel, carries one of the most-used transfer portraits of the King. Unmarked. £65 ($95–100)

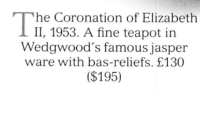

𝓔LIZABETH II

The Coronation of Elizabeth II, 1953. A fine teapot in Wedgwood's famous jasper ware with bas-reliefs. £130 ($195)

The Coronation of Elizabeth II, 1953. A splendid example of royal commemorative kitsch: a gilded pottery teapot in the shape of the State or Coronation Coach bearing a transfer of the Queen in uniform at the Trooping the Colour Ceremony. By Garden House Pottery. £75 ($110–115). (Similar teapots, in cream pottery, lightly gilded and with different transfers were made by Thomas Hughes.)

The Coronation of Elizabeth II, 1953. A gilded pottery teapot decorated in thin "good taste" in the style of the 1951 Festival of Britain. By Lingard. £75 ($110–115)

The Wedding of Prince Charles and Lady Diana Spencer, 1981. Although the shape and transfer on this pottery teapot are rather pedestrian, few royal commemorative teapots were made by this date, so it is of interest. By Price of Kensington. £20 ($30)

GEORGE VI

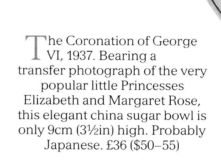

The Coronation of George VI, 1937. Bearing a transfer photograph of the very popular little Princesses Elizabeth and Margaret Rose, this elegant china sugar bowl is only 9cm (3½in) high. Probably Japanese. £36 ($50–55)

ELIZABETH II

China thimbles have been made to mark many royal events over the years and are particularly popular, not least with thimble collectors. This selection marks events involving the Prince and Princess of Wales and their young sons.

The Birth of Princess Eugenie of York, 23 March 1990. Bell's Distillery have commissioned such china bottles or decanters of their "Old Scotch Whisky" for a number of royal events since 1981. By George & Son Ltd. £25 ($35–40)

GLASS

Although not made for a specific royal event, a crystal goblet engraved with scenes of a hunt, the name Dier and the date 1581 is the first known piece of English glass to carry the Royal Arms – those of Elizabeth I. This goblet is of special interest to collectors because, as Elizabeth II's accession in 1952 was hailed as a "New Elizabethan Age", copies of the "Dier" goblet were made for general sale and are well worth looking out for.

Although it was not made to commemorate an important royal occasion, the "Exeter Flute", an elegant 43cm (17in)-high glass so called because it was probably given to Charles II at a banquet held in his honour by the Mayor of Exeter, is one of the earliest of royal commemoratives, carrying an engraved portrait and the words "God Bless King Charles the Second".

The first piece of glass made to mark an important royal event, the accession of William and Mary in 1689, is a crystal goblet engraved with the arms of William III and inscribed "God Bless the King". Such a piece, hand-blown and hand-engraved, was not made for the general public, any more than were other goblets made for successive coronations up to William IV's in 1821. But an important change in glass production was on the way.

GLASS FOR ALL

Although pressed or moulded glass had been made in small quantities since Egyptian times, it was not until the 1820s that the process was perfected, making mass production possible. The method, invented in the U.S., arrived in England in 1830 and soon thousands of cheap imitations of hand-blown objects were made for people who could not afford the real thing.

Queen Victoria's coronation in 1838 therefore saw the first examples of pressed glass commemoratives, mostly plates and saucers decorated with a portrait, her name and symbols.

Victoria's Golden Jubilee in 1897 witnessed the greatest number of glass pieces made for a royal event. About 100 different items, such as plates of every size, saucers, bowls, dishes, jugs, covered urns, tumblers, beakers, baskets, candlesticks and even photograph frames, were produced. The designs were mostly carried out in a new impressed-dot technique which created a brilliance that had not been possible in hand-blown glass on clear, amber, amethyst, blue and yellow glass.

One particular large and heavy clear-glass plate or dish, bearing an inscription and a crown and dating from 1887, has been produced virtually unchanged (except for different names and dates) for subsequent jubilees and coronations up to Elizabeth II. Variations include plates on which the monarch's and/or consort's heads are gilded or printed on paper in colour and stuck to the back of the plate; similar coloured-glass plates were also made.

"Economy" and Expensive Markets

Numberless cheap, usually unmarked clear, coloured or moulded glass items, mostly decorated with white or coloured transfers, have been made to commemorate many royal events. However, most of the major glass manufacturers have also produced a number of fine, hand-blown and hand-decorated pieces. For Edward VIII's "proposed" coronation, Stuart Crystal issued a large cut and engraved crystal bowl and an engraved tankard which, with changed cypher, they repeated for George VI's coronation. In line with James Kent Pottery's "Year of the Three Kings" tyg (see page 12) Royal Brierley Crystal issued its own "Three Kings" decanter.

For Elizabeth II's coronation the same firm made a "Three Queens" decanter; its three sides bearing the monograms of Queen Mary, 1911, Queen Elizabeth (later, the Queen Mother), 1937, and the Queen, 1953. One of the most elegant and coveted of Brierley's expensive pieces, made in 1953, is their "Commonwealth Cup", a loving cup engraved with the royal cypher and emblems of the Commonwealth countries.

Among Stuart Crystal's contributions to this coronation was their first limited edition piece: a tall, engraved vase which cost £20 ($30) – a lot of money in those days, and worth far more today. However, the same firm also issued "economy" tumblers etched with the royal cypher; they cost only 39s (nearly £2 [$3]) a dozen.

A "Cinderella" Coach

Glass paperweights have long been popular royal commemorative pieces. The first known example, faceted and with an embedded cameo portrait of Queen Victoria, was made in about 1838. A similar pair of weights bearing cameo portraits of the Queen and the Duke of Edinburgh was made for the Silver Jubilee of 1977, an event for which more than 60 different glass pieces were issued, including goblets, bowls and mirrors. They ranged in price from £1 ($1.50) for tankards to £675 ($1000 plus) for one of the most extraordinary glass commemoratives ever made. It is a 60cm (2ft)-long faithfully modelled replica of the State or Coronation Coach, complete with eight horses, traces and harness.

A Special Birthday

A number of good glass pieces were made to mark the Queen Mother's 90th birthday. Stuart Crystal's goblet has an air-twist stem and bears the Queen Mother's personal Royal Arms; it also carries the Imperial State Crown, an error, because this piece is never worn by a Queen Consort. Michael Virden made a crystal glass bell engraved with Elizabeth of Glamis roses that were named after her, a compliment which must have pleased Her Majesty.

VICTORIA

Queen Victoria's Golden Jubilee, 1887. One of the many dot-impressed pieces of pressed glass made to mark this event, 12.4cm (5in) in diameter, it was also made in a number of colours. Unmarked. £20 ($30)

GEORGE V

The Silver Jubilee of George V, 1935. A heavy tankard which carries moulded portraits of the King and Queen Mary against a background of the Union Jack and laurel leaves. By Sowerby of Gateshead. £15 ($20–25)

GEORGE VI

The Coronation of George VI, 1937. A fine, rib-bordered plate, bearing an embossed and gilded inscription and profiles of the King and Queen Elizabeth set in a circle of national flowers. Unmarked. £18 ($25–30)

The Coronation of George VI, 1937. Simple inexpensive tumblers with white or coloured transfer prints were sometimes, as here, bought by publicans to distribute as advertisements to the pub's customers. An added stencilled missive reads: "SOUVENIR FROM MR & MRS TED BLYTH THE COLLEEN BAWN". Unmarked. £8 ($12)

The Coronation of George VI, 1937. Virtually unchanged in design since 1887, this scallop-edged dish is embellished with moulded and dot-impressed decoration. Unmarked. £15 ($20–25)

ℰLIZABETH II

The Investiture of the Prince of Wales, 1969. A heavy tankard embellished with an embossed Prince of Wales badge. By Dartington. £15 ($20–25)

The Wedding of Princess Elizabeth and Lieutenant Philip Mountbatten, 1947. Because of post-war austerity, very few commemoratives were made to mark the marriage of the future Elizabeth II and the Duke of Edinburgh. This two-sided handbag mirror with photographic portraits of the couple is therefore a rare piece. Unmarked. £15 ($20–25)

The Coronation of Elizabeth II, 1953. *Left:* a popular gilt-rimmed tumbler decorated with a transfer print. Unworked. £5 ($7.50). *Right:* also gilt-rimmed and transfer-decorated, this somewhat grander goblet has a red glass knob. By Webb Corbett. £12 ($15–20)

The Investiture of the Prince of Wales, 1969. An 8.5cm (3⅛in)-diameter paperweight, beautifully decorated with an intaglio Prince of Wales badge and lettering. By Dartington. £12 ($15–20)

The Coronation of Elizabeth II, 1953. An ashtray decorated with a photograph of the Queen at the Trooping the Colour ceremony. Unmarked. £12 $(15–20)

METALS

So many commemoratives have been made in precious and base metals that they form a particularly interesting field for collectors.

MEDALS

From Edward VI's coronation in 1547 to William IV's in 1821, officially struck gold, silver and copper medals were distributed to members and servants of the Royal Household, to those attending the ceremony in Westminster Abbey and to the small crowd gathered in Abbey Yard. At Queen Victoria's coronation in 1838, the custom was abandoned and, up to George VI's coronation in 1937, such medals were for sale.

As with other commemoratives made for Edward VII's 1902 coronation, medals can carry either the "incorrect" 16 June date or the "correct" 9 August one, making the latter quite rare. Since then, rising costs, a fall in the general status of medals and an increased interest in philately have meant that the number of official coronation medals has decreased. Indeed, government advisors imagined that there would be no demand for medals to commemorate Elizabeth II's coronation in 1953, and none at all were made. However, the Royal Mint, realising late in the day that there would have been interest, hastily issued a number of inexpensive presentation medals which were given chiefly to schoolchildren. During the present Queen's reign, the Royal Mint and Spink and Son, the royal medallists, have issued a number of gold, silver and silver-gilt medals for such events as the Queen's Silver Jubilee in 1977 and the Queen Mother's 90th birthday.

Since the reign of George III, cheap base-metal medals, usually made to hang on chains or to be pinned on clothes, and even cheaper pin-on badges, have been issued for every possible royal occasion.

COINS

In 1953, to attract royalists and collectors, the Royal Mint struck the first of a series of commemorative crown or five shilling (25p) pieces. Since then, not necessarily for a particular royal event, the Mint has also issued boxed Proof Sets consisting of a number of different-value coins which make good collectors' items.

SILVER AND PEWTER

The majority of silver commemoratives are not only rather expensive but usually very conventional: the only royal decoration being small *repoussé* portraits or engraved Royal Coats of Arms. For the Silver Jubilee years of George V and Queen Elizabeth II, representations of their heads were added to hallmarks; these are often the only sign that a piece is a commemorative at all. Silver plate and pewter commemoratives – the latter most often in the form of tankards – are, of course, much cheaper. Silver, pewter or gilt replicas of the coronation regalia, in particular the Anointing Spoon, are of special note.

ENAMELLED BEAKERS AND MUGS

The first British enamelled tin royal commemorative beaker was made for Queen Victoria's Diamond Jubilee in 1897. (Three enamelled teapots were also issued.) Similar beakers and mugs, decorated with portraits, first drawn, then photographic, have been made to mark many royal events since. Of particular interest is a beaker made in 1977 to mark the Diamond Jubilee of the House of Windsor and the Septicentenary of the town of Windsor. Made by Halcyon Days, a London antique shop famed for making modern enamelled pieces, it is in design and finish a cut above the usual enamelled beakers.

TINS

Although producers of perishable goods had been putting their wares in tins since the 1840s, it was not until Queen Victoria's Golden Jubilee of 1897 that they realised that a royal image on a tin would greatly help sales – resulting in a proliferation of such tins up to the present day.

Victorian royal tins are not easy to find, but look out for a "Soldiers of the Queen" biscuit (cookie) tin of 1897, featuring portraits of the young and old Queen and her troops, and a small tin box for chocolates

carrying the Queen's portrait, which was sent as a New Year gift in 1900 to troops fighting the Boer War of 1899–1902.

Tins made to mark early royal weddings are particularly rare and sought-after: for the Duke and Duchess of York (later George V and Queen Mary), 1893; for the Princess Royal and Viscount Lascelles, 1922; and for the Duke and Duchess of York (later George VI and Queen Elizabeth), 1923. One of the most unusual – similar to the teapot on page 00 – is a Coronation Coach-shaped tin made to mark the accession of Edward VIII in 1936.

BRASS

The best-known commemoratives in this material are horse brasses bearing portraits, crowns and sometimes inscriptions. There are also trays, ashtrays, bells and spoons as well as some oddities which border on the kitsch. These include, in addition to those illustrated here, an 1897 trivet in the shape of a crown; Edward VII on horseback as a doorstop; doorknockers bearing royal portraits, and a pair of bookends in the shape of Edward VIII's profile.

A MISCELLANY

The most usual metal commemoratives are spoons; made of silver and in all kinds of base metals, they are often enamelled. The cheap ones were a favourite present for children. Then there are tin trays, money boxes in various metals, lead State or Coronation Coaches and even an aluminium cigar tube made for Elizabeth II's coronation.

MEDALS

Queen Victoria's Golden Jubilee, 1887. A white metal medal on which the Queen wears a miniature coronet and veil. Unmarked. £5 ($7.50)

The Coronation of Edward VII, 1902. A beautifully modelled official bronze medal, in direct line since 1547, carrying the "correct" date of 9 August. The reverse carries an equally fine portrait of Queen Alexandra. The Royal Mint. £30 ($45) in original case.

The Coronation of George VI, 1937. A gilt base-metal medal. By Thomas Fattorin Ltd. £3 ($4.50)

The Silver Jubilee of Elizabeth II, 1977. A silver-gilt medal in its original plastic case. The Royal Mint. £3 ($4.50)

BADGES

The "Proposed" Coronation of Edward VIII, 1937. A range of metal badges in the original box. They would probably have been sent by the wholesaler to a retailer to be sold separately. Unmarked. £10 ($15)

Badge for the Silver Jubilee of George V, 1935.

Badge for the Wedding of Prince Charles and Lady Diana Spencer, 1981. Unmarked. £2 ($3)

Badge for the Coronation of George VI, 1937. Unmarked. £2 ($3) each.

ENAMELLED BEAKER AND MUG

Badge for Silver Jubilee of Elizabeth II, 1977. Unmarked. £2 ($3)

COIN

The Wedding of Prince Charles and Lady Diana Spencer, 1981. A silver crown (25p) piece in its original plastic case; as it is legal tender, it carries a portrait of the Queen on the reverse. Made by the Royal Mint but issued by the Trustee Savings Bank. £1 ($1.50)

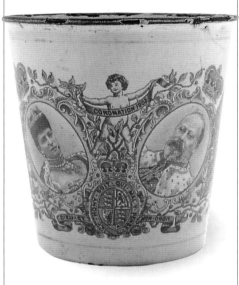

The Coronation of Edward VII, 1902. An enamelled tin beaker. Probably made by the Russian firm B.G. Gottieh, which exported to British firms. Unmarked. £40 ($60)

The Coronation of Elizabeth II, 1953. An enamelled mug which, as far as is known, is the only commemorative for this event to carry this transfer. Made by Kendrick in their "Anglo" brand Enamel Ware. £18 ($25–30)

TINS

The Coronation of Edward VII, 1902. A tiny 6cm (2⅝in)-diameter gilded and silvered tin for Mazawattee Chocolate. Unmarked. £8 ($10–15)

The Coronation of George V, 1911. A chocolate or cigarette tin. Issued by the Honourable Society of Lincolns Inn, bearing its badge. Unmarked. £16 ($20–25)

Edward, Prince of Wales. Probably made in the 1920s; this fine biscuit (cookie) tin carries views of places in the British Empire around the base, a tribute to the Prince's popular tours. Such tins are particularly sought-after. Unmarked. £20 ($30)

The Silver Jubilee of George V, 1935. Probably a biscuit (cookie) tin. Unmarked. £12 ($15–20)

The Coronation of George VI, 1937. An unusual embossed tin, probably for biscuits (cookies). Unmarked. £10 ($15)

expensive marble, Parian (named after the Greek island of Paros where marble had been quarried) porcelain was created in about 1845. Generally white and with a translucent surface, it was a fair imitation, and soon became very popular, mainly for figurines and busts. Few royal figurines or busts appear to have been made until Queen Victoria's Jubilees. In miniature crown or veil-only versions, these busts ranged from 35.5cm (14in) high to as little as 16.5cm (6½in). Parian busts were also made for Edward VII's coronation and his death, and for the coronation of George V. For those who could not even afford these comparatively inexpensive Parian pieces, still cheaper plaster copies were also on sale, as were other plaster busts for coronations since then. From 1881 until at least 1911, small busts made by such crested-china firms as Goss and Arcadian China carried transfers of town crests.

Of note are Wedgwood's black basalt busts, such as the one made of Princess Elizabeth at the time of her father's coronation in 1937, which was reissued to mark her Silver Jubilee as Queen in 1977. Although Parian was, by then, more expensive to produce, to commemorate the wedding of the Prince of Wales and Lady Diana Spencer in 1981, Poole Ltd made a pair of 11.5cm (4½in)-high Parian busts with Prince of Wales feathers in relief on the back of each.

PLAQUES

Here again, the range of materials is wide – from china to cardboard. Plaques can be round, oval and rectangular and, during the Art Deco period, carried "face" portraits. (Similar ones had been made in brass and steel of Queen Victoria and Prince Albert to celebrate their wedding in 1840.) Probably for outdoor decoration, metal-faced cardboard shield-shaped plaques, 45cm (1ft 5⅞in) deep, were made for the "proposed" coronation of Edward VIII. The manufacturers claimed, ironically, as it turned out, that they would "last a lifetime and be a permanent souvenir of the Coronation".

MEDALLIONS

In Britain, royal portrait oval medallions date from about Queen Anne's reign, 1702–1714. In 1773 Josiah Wedgwood issued a number of basalt and bisque medallions of "Illustrious Moderns" followed in 1779 by the first of his famous blue and green and white ovals with beautifully modelled portraits, including George III and his consort Queen Charlotte. The firm has been making such medallions of members of the Royal Family ever since.

When the Duke of Windsor died in 1972, Wedgwood issued a black basalt medallion; it is a copy of the blue and white jasper version made to mark the visit of the Duke, then Prince of Wales, when he visited the factory in 1924. Both are very good collectors' items.

The Coronation of Edward VII, 1902. A 20.5cm (8in)-high bisque figurine of the crowned King, carrying the orb and a staff, wearing an ermine-lined and caped robe and the Garter chain, rather oddly, over a lounge suit! There would have been a matching figurine of Queen Alexandra. Unmarked, but signed *M.G.E. Flowske,* it is probably continental. £85 ($125–130)

For its size, only 7.8cm (3½in) high, this very well-modelled cast-lead figurine of Queen Elizabeth in her coronation robes is part of a set which includes King George VI and the Coronation Chair. By William Britain. £18 ($25–30). (A set: £50/$75.)

The Coronation of Edward VII, 1902. Prettily painted 35cm (12in)-high Staffordshire pottery figures of the King and Queen Alexandra; among the last to be made of royalty in this ware. Unmarked. £400 ($600) the pair.

The 90th Birthday of Queen Elizabeth, the Queen Mother, 1990. What more appropriate than that Royal Doulton, famed for its "lady" figurines since the 1930s and for its royal figurines, should produce this one to mark this special birthday of a much loved royal lady? Decorated with coloured enamels, the white china figurine stands 21cm (8½in) high and shows Her Majesty formally dressed, wearing the Garter sash and family honours, and carrying a ubiquitous royal handbag. It sold for £250 ($375), but may well go up in value.

*B*USTS

Queen Victoria's Golden Jubilee, 1887. Finely modelled Parian bust of the Queen wearing a veil and the Garter sash. Crowned versions were also made in this ware. 17cm (7in) high. By Turner and Wood. £120 ($180)

Queen Victoria's Diamond Jubilee, 1897. A tiny (only 7cm (2¾in) high) well-modelled and painted plaster bust of the regally dressed Queen. A similar version was made in Parian. With its painted wood plinth this piece is 16.5cm (6½in) high. Unmarked. £25 ($35–40)

The "Proposed" Coronation of Edward VIII, 1937. This plaster bust, a very good likeness of the King, is 20.3cm (8in) high and was probably also coloured. By Rocksyn. £25 ($35–40)

The Coronation of Edward VII, 1902. These finely modelled busts of the King and beautiful, bejewelled Queen Alexandra are plaster copies (they were also painted to resemble bronze) of those made in Parian by Robinson & Leadbeater. The Queen is 20.5cm (8in) high. £50 ($75) the pair.

George V and Queen Mary, 1922. Royal busts were not necessarily made to mark any particular event. These are in terracotta; the Queen is only 5cm (2in) high. Unmarked. £25 ($35–40)

George V, before 1936. A 7.5cm (3in)-high metal bust inscribed: "H.M. The King. A souvenir of Madame Tussauds". The famous wax museum issued many small metal busts of royal persons before the Second World War. Unmarked. £15 ($20–25)

The Coronation of George VI, 1937. These simply modelled and painted plaster busts – the King is 16.5cm (6½in) high – are in fairground style. Queen Elizabeth is erroneously given yellow hair and a curious chaplet. Unmarked. £25 ($35–40) the pair.

PICTURE POSTCARDS AND CIGARETTE CARDS

ogether with prints, picture postcards have done more than most other commemoratives to keep the royal image alive in relatively modern times. At the time of sale they did, and still do, cost very little, and even early examples – apart from some very rare or unusual ones – are still comparatively cheap.

Although we know the date of the world's first plain postcard: 1 October 1869, which was made in Austria, the date of the first wholly illustrated card is uncertain. It evolved slowly, in Europe, from small engraved black-and-white or single-coloured views to the first commemorative, a sketch issued to mark the Nuremberg Exhibition of 1 May 1882.

Because the British Post Office had a monopoly on plain postcards, Britain was slow to take up the challenge. Although, from 1870, the Post Office agreed to carry advertisements on some of its cards, it was not until 1894 that it allowed private firms to print their own. Few, however, took this advantage to produce pictorial cards until the Boer War of 1899–1901 when over 500 million pictorial postcards were issued in one year alone, succeeded by sepia and coloured, mainly topographical, cards.

At first, surprisingly, few cards depicted royalty – a rare coloured card of Queen Victoria for her 1897 Jubilee could cost as much as £150 ($225). But within 15 hours of the Queen's death on 22 January 1901, many "In Memoriam" cards, which now cost about £5 ($7.50) each, appeared, heralding a flood of royal cards which has never stopped.

Picture postcards have been issued to mark every possible royal event and to portray practically every member of the Royal Family over the years. Thousands of cards for Edward VII's coronation in 1902 were issued with the "incorrect" date, making those with the "correct" one rare. Tuck, enterprisingly, in the "Kings and Queens of England" series, reprinted a drawing of the King with the "incorrect" date obliterated, and gave away 100,000 cards as a charitable gesture. Cards for George V's coronation in 1911 are particularly imaginative; many show photographs of the King and Queen and/or their children superimposed on drawings of crowns or drapes.

Picture postcard firms have used every possible means of illustration: coloured drawings or paintings; black-and-white and sepia photographs; black-and-white photographs hand-coloured before reproduction, but cards printed from transparencies did not appear much before the 1950s. Cards were decorated with tinsel and embossed, and some most interesting ones are of the "concertina" (accordion) variety, with little flaps which, when opened, release a stream of tiny drawings or photographs (see the illustrations).

The most popular and/or better-looking members of the Royal Family have inspired the most cards. Beautiful and exquisitely dressed Queen Alexandra was a great favourite. She features on a number of cards made to mark Edward VII's death in 1910, but few were issued of her as Queen Mother. Queen Mary, also popular as Duchess of York, Queen Consort and Queen Mother, appears on many cards. The present Queen Mother, the most popular to hold that title, has also featured as Duchess of York and Queen Consort, portrayed in her inimitable style of dress.

Edward VIII – cards for his "proposed" coronation are prized – as Prince of Wales was the most popular and most photographed male member of the Royal Family ever; he appears on hundreds of cards, in boyhood sailor suit and, as an adult, in everything from uniforms to golfing gear. Reminding us of Queen Alexandra's beauty and sophistication, the present Princess of Wales has also proved a very popular subject for cards.

CIGARETTE CARDS

The first card to be included in a packet of cigarettes as a sales gimmick appeared in 1888. Since then, all the major tobacco firms have produced a multitude of subjects, in colour and black and white in vast numbers – between 1902 and 1940 some 300 million annually – but, oddly, few of royal subjects, which makes them among the rarest and, often, the most expensive of cigarette cards.

Early sets can be very pricey. Salmon & Gluckstein's set of six cards of "Her Most Gracious Majesty Queen Victoria" of 1897 could set you back £300 ($450); cards for Edward VII's coronation range in value from Players' set of six, now worth £270 ($400) to Wills' set of 50 worth £300 ($450). The same firm's 1935 Silver Jubilee set of 50 costs only £22.50 ($35), but George VI coronation cards range from £50 ($75) for a set of 50 coloured cards by Ogden to £2.50 ($4) for a black-and-white set of 50 by Players.

For those who thought that cards stuck into albums would be worth more than loose ones, the reverse is true. Because collectors – known as cartophilics – and dealers regard cards as "damaged" if they are stuck down, they are, therefore, worth about half the value of a loose set. But don't necessarily be put off buying albums; for the collector of royal commemoratives, an attractive filled album can be good to have – even if it *is* worth less than a loose set. (In some albums the cards are just inserted so they retain their loose value.)

The Coronation of George V, 1911. A fold-out postcard of the Coronation Chair, issuing forth 11 sepia photographs relating to the coronation. (Made in 1299, the Chair has been used for the crowning of every monarch, bar Mary I, since Edward II in 1308.) By Valentine. £2.50 ($3–4)

The Silver Jubilee of George V, 1935. Arranged to resemble a family tree, this set of 50 cigarette cards portrays members of the royal family and their ancestors. By Ardath Tobacco Ltd. £30 ($45)

The Coronation of Elizabeth II, 1953. A fold-out postcard, carrying 16 tiny coloured photographs illustrating scenes from the Queen's life. By Loggia Ltd. £2 ($3).

The Silver Jubilee of George V, 1935. A set of 50 coloured cards in an album, recording events in the King's reign. By W.D. & H.O. Wills. £11 ($15–20). (£22.50 ($30–40) loose.)

A selection of picture postcards: quite rare sepia photographs of George VI and Queen Elizabeth in their coronation robes, 1937, £15 ($20–25) the pair; a photograph of the Queen Mother in one of her famous hats, photographed by Tim Graham, £1 ($1.50); the Queen and the Duke of Edinburgh taking the salute at the Trooping the Colour Ceremony outside

Buckingham Palace, £1 ($1.50); an unusual card issued for the "proposed" coronation of Edward VIII drawn by Donald McGill, of seaside comic-postcard fame, £4 ($6); Queen Elizabeth II's Silver Jubilee, 1977, a photograph taken in Buckingham Palace by Baron Studios, kitschly decorated with a gilded metal crown, £1.50 ($2–3).

PORTRAIT PRINTS

As with postcards – and going farther back – popular prints, cheaply printed by a number of methods, have kept British royalty in the public eye; for centuries they have been acquired to frame and hang in the home, as they still are today.

From about Charles II's coronation in 1660 until the late 18th century, the only prints of royalty available to the general public were a few etchings and engravings.

In the late 18th century the invention of lithography, a method of printing drawings from stones, enabled more prints to be made and led, in the 1850s, to the production of some of the most popular and multifarious prints ever made: chromolithographs. Still using stones, one stone for each colour, and oil-based inks, it was possible to produce literally thousands of drawings, paintings and photographs – some printed on canvas-like paper to resemble oil paintings – many of them royal portraits.

Printed until at least George V's coronation in 1911 (see the illustration) they were sold loose or framed. As well as single ones of Queen Victoria for her 1887 Jubilee, pairs of herself and the Prince of Wales (later Edward VII) were also issued. From then until her death in 1901, group photographs and drawings of the Queen with her children, grandchildren and great-grandchildren were particularly popular.

Despite the enormous number made, the poorer-quality ones were generally not kept and chromolithographs are now quite scarce. Even the best, including those of royalty, are not easily found and can be expensive.

When, in 1890, half-tone or photogravure was first used commercially to print drawings, paintings and photographs in black and white, sepia and colour (at first from hand-coloured black-and-white photographs) for books, magazines and newspapers, the makers of royal prints had an even cheaper medium, with which they swamped the market. Their great opportunity came when, for Queen Victoria's 1897 Jubilee, they were able to issue black-and-white copies of two official photographs, often framed. In them, her 79-year-old face is heavily retouched (a common practice at this time for older people) to make her look younger and more romantic. In these photographs she wears a small diamond coronet, her wedding veil and an apron-like lace flounce over her black dress; in one photograph she holds a lace fan. These prints carry her signature and "January 1897" in her own hand – but don't be fooled into thinking that these are "real"; along with the photographs they are only reproductions. Other such prints, often coloured, were made of many other members of the British Royal Family and, since she was the "Grandmother of Europe", of continental royal families as well.

In the 1860s, when magazines and journals started to proliferate, the practice began of inserting free "Supplement" prints of royalty, sometimes for a special occasion, sometimes not. The custom increased the sale of such publications and continued until at least the Second World War.

MACHINE-WOVEN AND PRINTED FABRICS AND EMBROIDERY

Royal portraits, regalia, emblems, national flowers, Union Jacks, etc, have been machine-woven, printed and embroidered on everything from tapestries to bookmarks, from tea towels to T-shirts, giving the collector plenty of dignified and kitsch items to choose from.

MACHINE-WOVEN TEXTILES

Among the most sought-after – but not all that easy to find – woven silk portraits of royalty are called Stevengraphs. Thomas Stevens of Coventry, using a Jacquard loom, was already well established when, in the early 1870s, he began to make these pictures of many subjects, ranging from jockeys to royalty, measuring about 12.5 × 7.6cm (5 × 3in). Early royal pictures are scarce, as are those for Queen Victoria's Jubilees, but you might find some of Edward VII, Queen Alexandra, the Duke and Duchess of York – later George V and Queen Mary – singly or arranged in one mount. Other Coventry firms made Stevengraph-type portraits, often much larger, which are more easily found.

Stevens (and other firms) also made woven silk bookmarks featuring royalty. The tradition is still carried on: as recently as 1988 a pretty silk Jacquard example was made to celebrate the birth of Princess Beatrice of York.

From Queen Victoria's 1887 Jubilee onwards, various-sized machine-woven silk tapestries have

PRINCE OF WALES

been made for framing – see the illustration of one of George VI. For the 1977 Jubilee, a tapestry portrayal of Queen Elizabeth II, taken from Annigoni's 1955 portrait and measuring only 19 × 14cm (7½ × 5¾in), was machine woven in pure silk Jacquard by Cartright and Sheldon of Macclesfield. It cost as much as £56 ($80–85) at the time.

Among the other machine-woven items for the same event are pairs of lurex and acrylic women's socks decorated with Union Jacks and even a red, white and blue garter: all very kitsch.

PRINTED FABRICS

The earliest-known printed fabric commemorating a British royal event is a white silk handkerchief with a portrait and emblems in black, made to mark George III's Diamond Jubilee of 1809. Since then, a number of royal-event handkerchiefs, mostly in cotton, have been produced. Measuring from 66 × 58cm (26 × 23in) to 25.3cm (10in) square, they were intended to be framed or worn as headscarves. The first British headscarf proper seems to be a rare crêpe example made to mark Princess Elizabeth's wedding in 1947. For her coronation in 1953, as many as 18 differently designed handkerchiefs and 23 differently designed headscarves were produced in a range of materials such as cotton, silk, crêpe and linen; such scarves have been made for a number of royal events ever since. One of the most

interesting was issued to mark the wedding of the Duke of Windsor to Mrs. Simpson in 1937; it displays a sheet of music entitled "Dedicated to a Glorious Romance. Love, Life, Fate", portraits of the Duke and Duchess, and other famous historical and fictional lovers.

Various-sized royal portraits have been printed on silk for framing. Printed cotton flags, for indoor and outdoor decoration, include one made for Queen Victoria's 1897 Jubilee, titled "Four Generations of the Royal Family"; other coloured flags show the Queen encircled by the Royal Arms. Similar flags have been made for other coronations, among them those on which a dark blue portrait of the monarch is superimposed on a coloured Union Jack.

Items of clothing include little girls' dresses made of cotton printed with royal scenes and emblems, and T-shirts adorned with emblems or Union Jacks. The most kitsch of all must be a bra and brief set printed with the Queen's Silver Jubilee Appeal emblem which consists of a crown, the date and an inscription within a laurel-leaf wreath.

For the home, cotton or linen tea towels have been very popular: they are usually well decorated with royal and national emblems but no portraits. There are also some cotton tablecloths, aprons and a few oven mitts and teacosies.

EMBROIDERY

Samplers dating from the 16th century have been carried out mostly by children but, latterly, by adults as well, to commemorate a number of coronations. Most fairly modern examples of embroidery and "tapestry" work – in reality gros or petit point worked in wool on canvas – depicting portraits, the Royal Arms, etc, have been sold in kit form or as a transfer given away in women's magazines; intended to be framed or made into firescreens.

GEORGE VI

ELIZABETH II

The Coronation of Elizabeth II, 1953. One of the many heavy cotton printed flags made for decoration: a rather crude drawing of the Queen is superimposed on the Union Jack. British. 86 × 54cm (34 × 21½in). £5 ($8)

The Coronation of Elizabeth II, 1953. On this rayon headscarf the Queen is seen in uniform, set in a highly ornamental, Victorian-style cartouche. The border is made up of national flags and guardsmen. 83.5 × 76cm (33 × 30in). Made in Italy. £10 ($15)

The Coronation of George VI, 1937. Machine-woven silk tapestry, taken from a photograph. 39.5 × 30.5cm (15½ × 12in). There would have been a companion piece of Queen Elizabeth. Unmarked. In its original frame, £70 ($105)

EDWARD VIII

PRINCE OF WALES

Edward VIII as Prince of Wales, 1914–1918 Great War. Printed silk picture of the young Prince in the uniform of the Grenadier Guards. 16 × 12cm (6¾ × 4½in). Unmarked. £8 ($10–15)

The Wedding of the Prince of Wales and Lady Diana Spencer, 1981. A polyester headscarf which carries a rather amateur drawing of the couple, and, in the corners, two Prince of Wales Feathers badges as well as the arms of Wales and of the Duchy of Cornwall (Duke of Cornwall being one of the Prince's other titles). 68.8cm (27in) square. Unmarked. £8 ($10–15)

The Coronation of Elizabeth II, 1953. A printed glazed-cotton apron decorated with regalia, national flowers and Union Jacks. Unmarked. £10 ($15)

The Wedding of the Prince of Wales and Lady Diana Spencer, 1981. A cotton tea towel with a dignified if rather old-fashioned design with its Gothic lettering; it includes a drawing of St. Paul's Cathedral where the marriage was solemnised. By Vista. £5 ($7.50)

The Coronation of Elizabeth II, 1953. A sampler, probably worked by a little girl, which incorporates a coloured print of the Queen. 22 × 17.6cm (9½ × 7in). £8 ($10–15)

The Coronation of Elizabeth II, 1953. Set in an oval of national flowers, this embroidered portrait of the Queen is taken from a photograph by Dorothy Wilding. It would have been bought as a kit or been a transfer given away in a women's magazine. Contemporary frame: overall depth 25.5cm (10in). £18 ($25–30)

JIGSAW PUZZLES

Many people enjoy making jigsaws, and they have a longer history than most of us imagine and include many picturing royal subjects for the collector. They may be drawn or photographed, made for a particular (or no particular) event, or depict royal residences.

The first made to mark a royal event depicted the coronation procession of William IV and Queen Adelaide in 1831. In 1838 two puzzles portrayed Queen Victoria's coronation; they were followed by a few of herself, Prince Albert and their growing family.

Puzzles issued for the rest of Victoria's reign and up to George V's coronation in 1911 are hard to come by and are very expensive. By the end of the 19th century, even though some wooden puzzles were (and still are) made, wood was generally replaced by cardboard. The pieces were smaller and fully interlocking, and half-tone prints were used. Jigsaws were no longer instructional and only for children; from the late 1920s they were an adult "craze" and it is from the 1930s that most are found today.

In the 1930s, the little Princesses Elizabeth and Margaret Rose were favourite subjects: alone, or together outside the cottage given to them by the people of Wales, or visiting Ming the Panda at London Zoo. There are puzzles marking the weddings of three of George V's sons in the 1930s, but the most were made to celebrate his Silver Jubilee in 1935. The King is on his own or with Queen Mary, in their coronation robes or informally dressed, and with members of the Royal Family. The most striking of all is a reproduction of a painting by George Scott of the King in uniform astride his favourite horse, Kildare.

One of the most interesting made for Edward VIII's "proposed" coronation in 1937 is called "The First King to Fly": a photograph of the King as Prince of Wales in his flying gear. George VI's coronation inspired its batch of jigsaws: the monarchs in their full-length robes, in ovals; the King taking the Salute; and many depicting the coronation procession through London. Similar scenes were used on jigsaws for Elizabeth II's coronation in 1953 as well as portraits of herself, often crowned or with the Duke of Edinburgh.

The Duke also appears frequently on puzzles made for the Queen's Silver Jubilee in 1977: in the official photograph taken in Windsor Castle; with their children; and, on a double-sided puzzle that is difficult to make, he is in uniform on one side, and the Queen in glittering formal dress on the other. The Queen and the Duke, wearing the red robes of the Order of the British Empire, are seen leaving St. Paul's Cathedral and with the Royal Family on the balcony of Buckingham Palace. Cecil Beaton's famous photograph of the Queen in her robes was reissued – but printed the wrong way round!

Jigsaws were made to commemorate the weddings of the Prince of Wales and Prince Andrew, Duke of York and, in 1986, to mark the Queen's 60th birthday. A number of the Queen Mother's birthdays have also been marked, and several of the Princess of Wales have been issued since her marriage in 1981.

There are too many manufacturers to mention them all, but Waddington must be the most famous name. Jigsaws are particularly difficult to value since even some of the 1930s examples can be picked up for £10 ($15), yet one dealer in 1993 asked £495 ($750) for a depiction of Buckingham Palace!

The Coronation of Elizabeth II, 1953. This box contains an unusual circular puzzle showing the Queen and the Duke of Edinburgh in a formal photograph, with a drawing of the coronation procession around the border. By Waddington. £10 ($15)

The Coronation of George VI, 1937. A jigsaw puzzle displaying a painting of the King and Queen Elizabeth in their coronation robes. Maker unknown. £15 ($20–25)

Queen Elizabeth the Queen Mother's 80th Birthday, 1980. A charming informal photograph of the Queen Mother at home, probably at Clarence House. By Waddington. £5 ($7.50)

A ROYAL MISCELLANY

Books about royalty, whether for special occasions or not, are legion – a new one seems to come out every week. One of the strangest, and a real collectors' item, is the *Royal Family Pop-up Book* which appeared in 1985. Hardbound, with little text, it contains only five pages, with coloured illustrations of such occasions as the State Opening of Parliament and A Barbecue at Balmoral that pop up or can be moved by pulling or pushing tabs.

Countless special editions of magazines and journals have been published over the years. Of note are those issued by *The Illustrated London News* from the 1887 to the 1977 Jubilees. There are programmes and maps of coronation routes; Orders of Service for coronations and funerals; paper napkins recording Royal visits; brown paper bags and even specially printed writing paper. For the 1953 coronation, a paper parasol with a wooden handle and spokes displayed a portrait of the Queen and a Union Jack.

From Charles II's coronation in 1660 onwards, engraved, etched, lithographed and half-tone depictions of coronation processions have been printed on long, narrow strips; a number of them fastened into cylinders so that they can be rolled out. Telescopic views and peepshows date from at least Queen Victoria's coronation in 1838. For the 1953 coronation, Hulton Press issued *The Picture Post Coronation Peepshow Book,* which showed the scene in Westminster Abbey. In a telescopic view made for the 1977 Jubilee one can see the coronation procession making its way down the Mall from Buckingham Palace.

In jewellery, crown brooches, made in everything from diamonds to plastic, as well as other brooches, lockets, pendants, rings, cuff-links and collar-studs fashioned from all manner of materials and often containing little portraits, have always been popular.

Among beauty products a square metal powder compact with the King's portrait was made for the coronation of George VI in 1937, and for the 1953 coronation Helena Rubenstein issued a plastic powder box in the shape of a crown which held a jewelled lipstick case in the centre. While on the "sacrilegious" use of St. Edward's Crown, a 45.5cm (18in)-high cane replica, mounted on a velvet cushion, was made for the same coronation by one Charles Crampton, foreign relations representative of the British Matchbox Label Society for Messrs Dryad of Leicester. What were they thinking of?

Special playing cards, sold in packs of two, display a King and Queen separately on each pack or, in the case of Elizabeth II, herself on one, the Duke of Edinburgh on the other. At the time of George V's coronation in 1911, one could buy *Royal Coronation – The Game for all True Britons*. On a board, each player had to start from an Empire country and try to reach the coronation via Scotland, Wales, England or Ireland. What *fun* they must have had.

Dolls, probably not as playthings, depicting royals

have been made since Queen Victoria's coronation. For the 1977 Jubilee there were dolls of the Queen and the Duke of Edinburgh; a Royal Herald doll made of unbreakable styrene and dressed in a silk tabard; and a stuffed heraldic lion made of a plush material and wearing a crown.

Records, cassettes, videos and audio cassettes are, of course, relatively modern royal commemoratives. Probably the earliest and rarest record is that of Edward VIII making his abdication speech on radio on 11 December 1936, now worth about £40 ($60). The 1977 Jubilee was marked by a number of records (most of which were also issued as cassettes) such as one which played *Music from 25 Years of Royal Occasions*. Videos include the ITN programme *Diana. The Making of a Princess* shown in 1990 and the BBC's programme celebrating the 40th Anniversary of the Queen's accession to the throne in 1992. In August 1993, it was possible to buy an audio cassette of Andrew Morton's notorious book, *Diana: Her True Story* read by Stephanie Beacham with an introduction by the author, in contrast to the previous uncritical adulation of the Princess who was a partner in what was considered to be a "fairytale" marriage.

The most kitsch of all royal commemoratives, made for the 1953 coronation, must be an electric light bulb in which the element is twisted to form the royal cypher, topped by a crown.

The Coronation of Elizabeth II, 1953. A roll-out printed coloured drawing of the procession in a metal cylinder, equipped with a handle. Unmarked. £10 ($5)

The Coronation of Elizabeth II, 1953. A box of soap, each tablet embossed on both sides to resemble medals. By Joshua Mergerison. £8 ($10–15)

The Coronation of Elizabeth II, 1953. A charming, if rather kitsch, 4.5cm (1¾in)-deep metal brooch containing a photograph of the Queen embellished with clear and coloured brilliants. Unmarked. £8 ($10–15)

The Silver Jubilee of Elizabeth II, 1977. This record, *Elizabeth II. The Woman and the Queen*, contains BBC recordings of many occasions from the public and private life of Her Majesty. By Argo, a division of the Decca Record Company. £10 ($15)

The Wedding of Princess Anne and Captain Mark Phillips, 1973. A 43cm (17in)-deep, jolly plastic pennant with a fringe of man-made fabric. Unmarked. £5 ($7.50)

The Opening of the State Apartments of Buckingham Palace to the public, 1993. A paper carrier-bag from the souvenir shop – one of the smartest to be seen carrying in that and successive years! By Royal Enterprises Ltd. Given free but could be worth a few pounds eventually.

Elizabeth II and the Duke of Edinburgh, 1988. Stuffed, printed fabric slippers, 26.6cm (10in) long, with brown felt soles and plastic vinyl *Spitting Image* heads and hands. In Union Jack-covered "beds" the couple lie on pillows each embroidered with "H.R.H." – incorrect in the case of the Queen, which should be "H.M." Not since the late 18th and early 19th century have members of the Royal family been so caricatured and lampooned as in the puppets made by Fluck and Law for ITV's *Spitting Image* programme, first shown in 1984. (Similar slippers were made of the Prince and Princess of Wales.) By Linden Crafts and Gifts. £40 ($60) the pair.

SELECTED BIBLIOGRAPHY

DAVEY, M.H. & MANNION, D.J. *Fifty Years of Royal Commemorative China, 1887–1935.* (Dyman Publications, 1988)

DAVEY, M.H. & MANNION, D.J. *Four Generations of Royal Commemorative China,* 1936–1990. (Dyman Publications, 1991)

JACKSON, Josephine, *Fired for Royalty.* (Printed by Heaton Moor Printing Company, 1977)

JOHNSON, Peter, *Royal Memorabilia.* (Dunestyle Publishing Ltd, 1988)

KLAMKIN, Marion. *Picture Postcards.* (David and Charles, 1974)

ROGERS, David, *Coronation Souvenirs and Commemoratives.* (Latimer New Dimensions Ltd, 1975)

WARREN, Geoffrey, *Royal Souvenirs.* (Orbis Publishing, 1977)

ZEDER, Audrey, *British Royal Commemoratives.* (Wallace Homestead Book Co, Lombard, Illinois, USA, 1985)

𝒞 CATALOGUES ETC

THE CATALOGUE OF BRITISH AND FOREIGN CIGARETTE CARDS. The London Cigarette Card Company. Published yearly.

HERE'S A HEALTH UNTO THEIR MAJESTIES – Exhibition of Coronation Souvenirs from 1603–1953. Wolverton Art Gallery and Museums, 1973.

JOURNALS of The Commemorative Collectors Society, 1974–1993.

JUBILATION – Exhibition of Commemorative Pottery 1660–1935 from James Blewitt Collection, at Bethnal Green Museum, 1977,

JUBILEE ROYAL – a history of previous Royal Jubilees and a review of items issued to commemorate the Silver Jubilee of Elizabeth II. The Commemorative Collectors Society, 1977.

A PRINCESS FOR WALES – Royal Wedding Exhibition by the Commemorative Collectors Society, The Guildhall, Windsor, 1981.

A SELECTION OF DEALERS IN COMMEMORATIVE ITEMS

In alphabetical order under each heading, this list, apart from some dealers known to the author, is not to be taken as a personal recommendation or endorsement.

LONDON

Other than those listed in the acknowledgements

BRITTANIA ANTIQUES. (Ian and Rita Smythe) c/o Gray's Antique Market, 58 Davies Street, W1. Tel: 071 629 6772. *General commemoratives*

MR. PETER CLARK. 66 Lancaster Road, N4 4PT. Tel: 071 263 1564. *Victorian pressed glass.*

DAVID DRUMMOND AT PLEASURES OF PAST TIMES. 11 Cecil Court, WC2N 4EZ. Tel: 071 836 1141. *Postcards.*

LEGACY. Units 50 & 51, Alfie's Antique Market, 13–25 Church Street, NW8 8DT. Tel: 071 723 0449. *General commemoratives.*

MISS JOCELYN LUKINS. 14 Keith Grove, W12 9EZ. Tel: 081 749 5985. *Doulton commemoratives. Postal service – callers by appointment only.*

PAMELA AND DEREK RANSLEY. Stand No 25a–27a, Westbourne Arcade, 113 Portobello Road, W11. Tel: 0424 882838. *General commemoratives, mainly antique and ceramics.*

BRITISH ISLES

AMBASSADOR BOOKS. 19 Reading Road, Henley-on-Thames, Oxon, RG9 1AB. Tel: 0491 575432. *Mainly recent books, printed ephemera e.g. calendars, jigsaw puzzles, videos.*

A. BUCKINGHAM LTD. (Mr A. Buckingham) Benham House, The Bayle, Folkestone, Kent CT20 1SD. Tel: 0303 850041. *Postcards.*

CEE-EMM ENTERPRISES. 5 Shrubbery Hill, Cookely, Worcestershire DY10 3UW. *SAE for annual list of postcards only.*

CHARTERHOUSE ANTIQUES. (Mr A. & Mrs S. Webster) 1b Northumberland Place, Teignmouth, South Devon. Tel: (evening) 0626 54592. *General commemoratives.*

CROWNS AND SCEPTRES. (Mrs C. M. Watkinson), 146 Kestral Park, Skelmersdale, Lancs WN8 6TA. Tel: 0695 28601. *General commemoratives. Lists every two months – UK only £2.50 per copy or £12.50 per year.*

ENTERPRISE POSTCARDS. (Jill Willmott), 9 Quarry Road, Hanham, Bristol BS15 2PA. Tel: 0272 607154.

GOVIER AND SON LTD. (Mr A. Morgenroth), 55 High Street, Sidmouth, Devon EX10 8LN. Tel: 0395 578201. *Exclusive ceramics, mainly Royal Crown Derby porcelain. Mail-order brochures available.*

MR MARTIN R. G. HANDS. Stratford-on-Avon Antique Centre, Ely Street, Stratford-on-Avon, Warwickshire. Tel: 0789 68861. *Ceramic commemoratives.*

MRS L. M. HODGSON. Cuckoo Cottage, Main Street, Great Longstone, Nr Bakewell, Derbyshire DE45 1TA. Tel: 0629 640468. *General commemoratives.*

MR R. HUNT. 6 Alford Road, Heaton Chapel, Stockport, Cheshire SK4 5AW. Tel: 061 442 0276. *Printed ephemera, jigsaws, medals, horse brasses etc. Sends lists.*

MR F. D. AND MRS R. F. LEWIS. 20 Peace Road, Stanway, Colchester, Essex CO3 5HT. Tel: 0260 571491. *Ceramic commemoratives.*

LION AND UNICORNS COMMEMORATIVE CHINA. (Mrs J. Pearson), Kiltearn House, Hospital Street, Nantwich, Cheshire CW5 5RL. Tel: 0270 628892. *General commemoratives – mail order service and lists.*

MRS G. MANNION, 53 Lynn Road, Terrington St. Clement, King's Lynn, Norfolk PE34 4JU. Tel: 0553 828 887. *Ceramic commemoratives.*

MIDLANDS GOSS AND COMMEMORATIVES. (Betty and Nevil Malin), c/o Warwick Antiques Centre, 22 High St, Warwick CV34 4AP. Tel: 0926 495704. *Mainly ceramic commemoratives and Goss. Special facilities by post.*

MRS A. MINNS. Pelham House, 13 Dudley Road, Ashford, Middlesex TW15 2LG. Tel: 07842 54155. *General commemoratives.*

RAYMER COLLECTORS CENTRE. Barum House, 5 Bear St, Barnstaple, Devon EX32 7BU. Tel: 0271 45581. *General commemoratives – including books and postcards.*

RECORD AND CASSETTE CENTRE. (J & L Harris), 64 Preston New Road, Blackpool, Lancashire FY4 4HG. Tel: 0253 65001. *Records and cassettes.*

PETER AND SUSAN REES. 20 Green Lane, Stopsley, Luton, Bedfordshire. Tel: 0582 715555. *General commemoratives.*

ROYALTY DIGEST (Mr Paul B. Minet), Old Knowle, Frant, Kent TN3 9EH. Tel: 0892 750201, *Monthly journal; 19th and 20th century general commemoratives.*

RUNNERZ (Peter Grey), 10 Linden Drive, Prestatyn, Clwyd, North Wales LL19 9EH. Tel: 0745 853501. *General commemoratives. Mail order only – lists £1 UK. US: $2.*

THE SUSSEX COMMEMORATIVE WARE CENTRE. (Mrs R. Prior), 88 Western Road, Hove, East Sussex BN3 1JB. Tel: 0273 773911. *General commemoratives, including postcards. Six catalogues annually. £3 each or $7 Air Mail.*

THE STRAIT ANTIQUES. (Mrs F. N. Davies), 5 The Strait, Lincoln, Lincolnshire LN2 1JD. Tel: 0522 23130. *Commemorative ceramics.*

PAUL WYTON. "Uplands", Uplands Avenue, Caister-on-Sea, Great Yarmouth, Norfolk NR30 5JU. Tel: 081 863 0625 or mobile phone 0860 781386. *Commemorative china. Overseas mail provided.*

USA

A TOUCH OF BRITAIN (Rose and Bill Firth), Tiffany House, Penn's Market, Route 202, PO Box 3, Lahaska, Pennsylvania 18931. Tel: 215 794 0234. *Commemorative china, glass, silver.*

SIS BECKER. 14459 Lawndale Avenue, Midlothian, Illinois 60445. *British Royalty items – USA only. Twice-yearly lists.*

BRITISH ROYALTY COMMEMORATIVES (Mrs Audrey B. Zeder), 6755 Coraline, Long Beach, CA 908080. Tel: 310 421 0881. *Antique and modern commemoratives. Mail Order "For Sale" Commemorative List: $3 USA and Canada; £2 UK.*

SALLY CARVER, 179 South St, Chestnut Hill, MA 02167. *Postcards.*

CROWN ANTIQUES (Mr Peter J. McGechie), International Antiques Center, 2300 W. Diversey, Chicago, Illinois 60647. Tel: 312 227 2400. *General commemoratives from Queen Victoria to Elizabeth II.*

EVERYTHING ROYAL (Alicia Carroll), PO Box No. 48796, Los Angeles, California 90048. Tel: 213 655 1458. *General commemoratives. SAE for list.*

HYDE PARK ANTIQUE CENTER. Case no S-19, Hyde Park, New York. *General Commemoratives.*

MAN-TIQUES LTD (Mrs E. Zelin), 1050 Second Avenue, Gallery 51, New York 10022. Tel: 212 759 1805. *General commemoratives.*

J. DAVID McCLAIN, 7117 Rockwood Road, Little Rock, Arkansas 72207. Tel: 501 666 7090. *General commemoratives. Mail Order only.*

ELVA S. MYLROIE, R.D. No. 3, Amsterdam, New York 12010. Tel: 518 399 9598. *Mainly ceramic commemoratives.*

RAINY DAY BOOKS (Frank and Lucia Bequaert), PO Box No. 775, Fitzwilliam, NH 03447 0775. Tel: 603 585 3448. *Books and ephemera.*

ROYAL FOCUS (Victoria Evrard), PO Box No. 11198, Oakland, CA 94611. Tel: 510 420 1290. *Books, magazines, ephemera, jigsaw puzzles, videos etc.*

ROYAL GEMS (Sheryl Mashinskie), R.F.D. No. 1, PO Box No. 910, Plainfield, Vermont 05667. Tel: 802 426 3318. *Commemorative china, printed items, tins etc.*

ROYALTY BOOK SHOP (Dr Wayne S. Swift), Suite No. 803, 30 East 60th Street, New York, NY 10022. Tel: 212 758 3351. *Books and ephemera.*

ROYALTY SALES (Marcia L. Petersen-Walther), 1062 N.W. Keasey, Roseburg, Oregon 97470. Tel: 503 672 8078. *General commemoratives.*

UPSTAIRS, DOWNSTAIRS (Daisy F. Banks), 4 Houghton Point North, Swanzey, New Hampshire 03431. Tel: 1 603 352 7231. *General commemoratives. Mail order only.*

JOHN WIENEMAN, 1106 Major Drive, Jefferson City, MO 65101. Tel: 314 634 2351. *General commemoratives. Mail Order only.*

CANADA

NEXT IN LINE ROYAL COMMEMORATIVES (Lisa Mitchell), 264 Scarborough Road, Toronto, M4E 3M8. Tel: 416 699 2480. *General commemoratives. Catalogue $3 or £2.*

ROYAL BOOKS (Mr D. Martin), Suite No. 214, 2650 Southvale Crescent, Ottawa, Ontario, Canada K1B 4S9. *Books, magazines, ephemera. Mail Order catalogues.*

SUSSEX ANTIQUES (Don and Pat Peters) 435 East Columbia St, New Westminster, British Columbia V3L 3X4. Tel: 521 1322. *General commemoratives.*

AUCTION HOUSES

W. & F. C. BONHAM & SONS LTD. Montpelier St, London SW7 1HH. Tel: 071 584 9161. *Specialised commemorative sales.*

ANDREW MILTON, SPECIAL AUCTION SERVICES. The Coach House, Midgham Park, Reading, Berkshire RG7 5UG. Tel: 0734 712949. *Regular auctions of commemoratives.*

PHILLIPS SON AND NEALE. Collectors Department, 10 Salem Road, London W2 4DL. Tel: 071 229 9090. *Regular sales of commemoratives.*

SOCIETY

THE COMMEMORATIVE COLLECTORS SOCIETY. Honorary Secretary: Steven N. Jackson, 25 Farndale Close, off Wilsthorpe Rd, Long Eaton, Nr Nottingham, NG10 3PA. Tel: 0607 667666. Ordinary Membership per year: UK: £12. USA $25. Canada: £15. Members receive journals and any special publications.